Kids Helping Kids

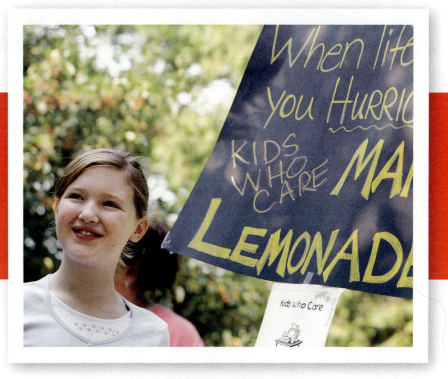

by Ernst Kelley

Glenview, Illinois • Boston, Massachusetts • Chandler, Arizona
Upper Saddle River, New Jersey

Hurricane Katrina hits the Gulf Coast.

In August of 2005, a strong hurricane hit parts the southern United States. It raced across the Gulf of Mexico, getting bigger every hour. When the storm came on land, there were huge waves, heavy rains, and powerful winds.

Many people left the area before the storm hit. But many people were at home or at work when the hurricane reached land.

Hurricane Katrina destroyed homes and buildings.

The storm had a big impact on the city of New Orleans, Louisiana. Ocean water flooded the streets. Winds blew off roofs and broke windows. The hurricane destroyed homes and buildings. Many people were scared.

Thousands of families moved to other states. Children had to go to school in new places.

All around the world, people wanted to help the people of New Orleans. But what could children do to help?

---

impact: to have an effect on

Kids in Chicago raise money for Katrina victims.

There are many examples of how children helped the victims of Katrina. In Chicago, Illinois, a group of children called "Kids Who Care" sold lemonade. They raised almost $2,000 in the two weekends after Katrina.

Two brothers in Massachusetts set up their own lemonade stand. They sent the money they made to victims of the hurricane.

At schools all across the country, children helped prepare food. They sent food and other supplies to the people in New Orleans.

---

victims: people who suffer from an accident, illness, or other bad event
supplies: things that people need

Children made signs to raise money.

In California, one 6-year-old boy raised almost $14,000! He made a sign asking people to donate to the American Red Cross. The Red Cross gives food and medical help to people.

At one school in Florida, a group of children sold beautiful necklaces. They used the money to help hurricane victims that were now going to their school. Many of these children had lost their homes.

Children sent backpacks full of supplies to Katrina victims.

Three sisters in Maryland—ages 8, 11, and 14—started a group called "Project Backpack." Thousands of people sent backpacks to help hurricane victims.

They called them "backpacks filled with love." Children wrote cards and letters. They drew pictures. They sent things they liked, such as toys and books. They sent school supplies. In one month, they sent 25,000 backpacks!

Children and businesses donated toys.

How old do you have to be to help? KJ Lewis from Nebraska was just five years old. He learned about Katrina and felt bad that so many children had lost their toys. He decided to send some of his own toys to the victims.

Then other people and stores in Nebraska donated toys, too. They collected 2,000 pounds of toys. A business paid for KJ and his mother to visit the children. KJ got to see them open their presents.

---

donated: gave something for a good cause

Kids can make a difference.

KJ brought a bicycle to one girl. The family expressed their gratitude to KJ.

"Well, it probably would be a bit different for a lot of people without the kindness and giving from KJ," said Byron Ottis, Sr.

How did KJ feel when he gave presents to the kids?

"It was just awesome!" he said.